LEEDS – THEN AND N

A photographic record of the twent... buildings of Leeds

By Brian Godward

CONTENTS

Introduction

Leeds Civic Trust has in the past published several books and booklets about the history and architecture of the city. Dr Derek Linstrum's *Historic Architecture of Leeds* and Dr Kevin Grady and Steven Burt's *Illustrated History of Leeds* are excellent appraisals of a long and rich heritage. On a lighter note, the fine *Old Leeds* series by Dorothy Payne presents an intriguing photographic record of a bygone age. However at this time for reflection at the Millennium it seems appropriate to consider in more detail architectural and town planning changes that have taken place in the city in the twentieth century.

THE TWENTIETH CENTURY IN LEEDS – AN OVERVIEW

Just over a century ago Leeds was granted city status, though it was 1903 before citizens could celebrate the opening of City Square, the symbol of its recognition. The period between 1890 and 1914 was a very busy one for the architects and builders. Such fine structures as the Markets, Arcades and the General Post Office arrived on the city scene, together with many banks, offices and hotels. Fortunately many of these survived the post-second world war building boom of the 1960s and 1970s and are key elements in today's city framework.

The first world-war and subsequent depression were perhaps instrumental in slowing down the pace of change between the wars, though great strides were made in slum clearance and the building of the large suburban estates. In the city centre the huge pioneering Quarry Hill Flats were linked to the Town Hall by the new Headrow, described by some as the 'Regent Street of the North'. White Portland stone was introduced to the city (and not without protest!) being used for several large buildings, notably the University, Queen's Hotel and forty years after city status, the majestic Civic Hall.

A virtual cessation of significant building activity in the city centre occurred between 1940 and 1960, caused by the war and subsequent stringent economic conditions. However in the suburbs council house building continued apace, priority again being given to re-housing people from slum-clearance.

It was in the early 1960s that the city began the process of major redevelopment, and it is probably fair to say that this continues to the present day (though the approach is vastly different!). Many early projects were on a huge scale entailing much demolition and a comprehensive approach alien to the local street scene. High office towers intervened on the skyline spoiling views and vistas with their bland architecture, seemingly based only on a desire for profitability. Leeds, of course, was not alone in this and, looking back, was probably better off than most other cities in retaining much of its historic fabric.

A FUTURE FOR THE PAST?

The Civic Amenities Act of 1967 and Conservation Areas were instrumental in making the public aware of the serious damage to the townscape being perpetrated by inconsiderate developers aided and abetted by officialdom. Now new developments could be considered with powers available to protect the old and cherished. Many local voluntary bodies were established in the 1960s in protest against the widespread destruction of towns and cities. Leeds Civic Trust was one of these, founded in 1965.

The process of conservation (rather than preservation) was introduced. This implies the substantial retention of older buildings through their adaptation for new uses without the loss of their original character. Cities, and their buildings, are in a continuous process of change over the years and need to adapt if they are to survive. In Leeds early examples of conservation include St Paul's House and the Bank of England, South Parade. In both cases only the fine facades were retained, the structures being gutted internally. Such an approach is today considered inappropriate. More recently fine examples of conservation include the Corn Exchange, Kirkgate Markets and the Victoria Quarter, all from the Victorian and Edwardian eras, but given a new lease of life.

Whilst conservation measures are probably universally popular with the public, what about the issue of new buildings? Controversy arose in the 1980s about the so-called "Leeds Look" for new buildings. It seemed that only those faced with red brick and roofed with slate received official sanction. They were usually of medium height and were mainly offices. Many people voiced the opinion that the Council was 'playing safe' and not encouraging invention and innovation, particularly since a wide range of new structural techniques and materials are now available to designers. Changes duly arrived in the 1990s and today a wide variety of building styles and design is evident. They offer contrast and interest in the street scene, with sheer walls of plate glass, marble, granite and (yes!) brick. City Square is vastly improved after the demolition of two 1960s horrors!

What the general public feels about modern buildings is often critical largely because change is difficult to accept. But change is inevitable, its been going on throughout the history of Leeds. Further, the pace of change is ever increasing as we enter a new Millenium. And, of course, that is the reason for this volume!

THEN AND NOW – THE CHANGING FACE OF LEEDS

The first part of the book concentrates on the changes to the architectural and town planning fabric and framework of the city made during the century. In some cases the changes brought about by redevelopment are quite striking, with little remaining of the original street scenes or buildings. East Parade and Park Street are examples where the new dominates leaving scant evidence of the past. However the city is fortunate in retaining many fine buildings from the past, saved from demolition by conservation, adaptation and sensitive re-use. Park Row House and Dyson's, Briggate are among those featured.

Street scenes have lost much of their visual (and perhaps romantic!) appeal particularly in the spaces between buildings, the highways and the pavements. The busy well-populated cobbled streets (even with tramlines) appear superior to the areas of bland yellow-lined grey tarmac required today. Not to forget the clutter of traffic signals, guard rails and the other impedimenta curiously known as street furniture (all to be seen on the newer photographs).

It has not always been possible to replicate exactly the viewpoints enjoyed by the original photographers. Change to road layouts and the installation of street furniture have sometimes called for a different approach. Heavy traffic flows at the wrong time of the day have often denied camera positions that only a foolhardy photographer might have risked! However it is hoped that the comparisons of "Then and Now" will either exult in enjoyment of the new or nostalgia for the past.

BUILDINGS OF THE CENTURY

The second part of the book concentrates on buildings of the twentieth century though in a few cases older structures are featured if they have been the subjects of change of use, conversion and conservation work. The title 'Buildings of the century' does not necessarily infer that particular examples are of a high architectural 'pedigree'. Some are listed and several more recent buildings have won Awards for Architecture in the City of Leeds scheme launched in 1987. The choice of the examples is subjective to a degree but the objective has been to illustrate the development of architectural styles, technology and materials through the years.

Buildings are arranged under a series of themes illustrating user types, for example education, hotels and banks. One obvious feature is that of the ever-increasing size and scale of structures. This is particularly evident in building types such as offices where the modest terracotta-clad Edwardian East Parade Chambers contrasts with the recent glass fronted 16 Park Row. Further, the modernistic Warner Village Multiplex Cinema is a far cry from the early beginnings of 'movies' in Leeds, in the Hyde Park.

CONCLUSION

Leeds has enjoyed a long post-war period of urban change and re-construction commencing over thirty years ago. Of course there have been some quiet periods, but the last decade of the century has witnessed an unprecedented building boom in this city. Even over the short period of months that this book has been in preparation a great deal of change has taken place. In consequence, apologies are due if some of the 'Now' views have changed slightly. But then 'freezing' the city is an impossible task. What will things look like in 2099? Maybe someone then will produce an appropriate and contemporary 'update' and I hope this volume will be a worthy record of the Twentieth Century in Leeds to which they can refer.

Brian Godward   *Autumn 1999*

City Square is seen shortly after its opening in 1903. *Left to right*, the GPO (1896), Standard Life Assurance Building (later Norwich Union), Priestley Hall (behind Black Prince), and Mill Hill Chapel. The GPO is listed Grade II (Architect – Henry Tanner), and the Chapel is Grade II*.

The scene in the 1970s, the Square is dominated by three high office buildings, the Norwich Union, NatWest, and Royal Exchange (the latter is out of the picture to the right).

The late 1990s see yet further changes. No. 1, City Square, replaces the Norwich Union and No. 1 Park Row is built on the former NatWest site. The Black Prince has retained its original siting but the layout of the rest of the Square was changed in the 1960s.

A 1950s view from City Square looking up Park Row, prior to the post-war building boom.

The rebuilding of City Square proved to be unpopular with many critics, the Norwich Union block (*left*) particularly disliked.

The view today with No. 1 Park Row on the right (Fletcher Joseph, Architects). Opposite, *on the left* is No. 1 City Square (Abbey Hanson Rowe, Architects). Developed by Norwich Union Investment Management the scheme was commended in the Leeds Awards for Architecture 1998.

A view from 1933 of the former Majestic Cinema and Ballroom in City Square which was built in the 1920s, an early forerunner of the entertainment places now common in the city today. The War Memorial was later moved to the Garden of Rest in Victoria Square on the Headrow so as to ease the growing problem of traffic congestion in City Square!

The 'Majestyk' as it is called today is in night club use. Much of the old signage has long gone and the entrance canopy is in a very different style of design. The building is listed Grade II, as is the Memorial. Architect for the building was P. J. Stienlet.

The view in the 1920s from City Square looking towards Boar Lane. *From left to right*, the former Royal Exchange building, Boar Lane, the former Midland Bank (now a pub-restaurant), and the former Queen's Hotel. The War Memorial was moved to the Headrow in the 1930s.

A recent view with the 1960s Exchange office tower on the left. The domed former bank remains in sharp contrast with its dominating neighbour. The Queen's Hotel of 1937 is seen on the extreme right of the photograph.

The view looking east along Boar Lane from its junction with Albion Street, a photograph from the 1930s. The busy street scene suggests much more variety in the shopping and trading than can be found today.

Today, this view of Boar Lane appears to have changed very little over the years with many of the original buildings retained and re-furbished. Perhaps the only 'modern' intervention is that of the C&A store (out of picture on left). The range of buildings on the right have been successfully restored to create the fine Trevelyan Square, including the Marriott Hotel.

A 1960s view looking west along Boar Lane from Briggate shows the C&A store prior to its redevelopment. The store was built in the early 1930s replacing a well-known Leeds 'institution' the 'Grand Pygmalion' the first department store in Leeds, opened in the 1880s, catering for the Victorian middle classes. It is interesting that all the other buildings on the photograph remain today albeit improved by refurbishment.

As part of the Trinity Street redevelopment the C&A store was constructed in the 1960s. Overhead walkway bridges were planned to cross Boar Lane into a new shopping centre on the south side but this never came to fruition.

A turn of the century view of the Corn Exchange (Cuthbert Brodrick 1862), one of the finest examples of Victorian commercial architecture in the country. Within this great space traders in cereals bought and sold their crops under the ideal natural daylighting provided by vast roof lights, designed so as to exclude direct sunlight (listed Grade I).

A 1960s view of the Corn Exchange, prior to cleaning and conservation.

In 1990, the Corn Exchange was restored and converted into a wide variety of shops, bars and restaurants on three levels, whilst retaining the magnificent character of the interior space. The architect was John Lyall for Speciality Shops. The conversion received an Award in the Leeds Awards for Architecture 1990.

A 1960s view of the interior of the Corn Exchange which at this time was only in occasional use, though some traders in cereals continued to operate here as they had done for over a century. The building was in need of considerable renovation.

A similar view after conversion in 1989. A hole was formed in the ground floor so as to open up basement storage, which is now a food court. Further stairs were added to give access to the first-floor balcony. Approximately 50 retail units were created on three levels. This photograph shows the physical changes described above and is not indicative of the normal busy shopping day when the space is laid out with stalls and displays.

John Dyson and Sons, the city's leading jewellers, clock and watchmakers since Victorian times traded from this elaborate shop in Lower Briggate until recently. 'Time Ball Buildings' was originally a simple Georgian-style house like its neighbours but received an ornamental facelift surmounted by the massive skysign late last century (listed Grade II*).

In a recent conversion to a restaurant (as part of the adjoining Marriott Hotel) Dysons was completely renovated and restored, both internally and externally. Diners now enjoy the splendid Victorian shop fittings, woodwork, etched glass and chandeliers. The skysign was not replaced, however. Architects for the original conservation works were Kitson and Partners. For the more recent project for Marriott Hotels in 1993 the architects were Cobban and Lironi. In 1994 the scheme received an Award in the Leeds Awards for Architecture.

The Royal Hotel, Lower Briggate, dates back to 1692 when it was known as the New King's Arms and coaches ran from here in 1765. It became the Royal in 1834 when it hosted the Royal Mail coaches. The building underwent many changes during its life and large underground stables were discovered when it was redeveloped in the late 1970s.

The building fell into disuse in the 1970s.

The Royal was rebuilt between 1979 and 1983. The frontage building, in a simplified form, serves as offices for a housing association. To its rear, Regent Court is a group of single person flats, an early example of the re-introduction of a resident population in the city centre.

A wartime view of Briggate from 1944 as seen from the Boar Lane junction. The busy scene shows few cars and many pedestrians. The largest 'new' building on the right was occupied by F. W. Woolworth opening in 1928 (*centre right* with large awning). The signs to such as Bradford and York on the lighting column (*right foreground*) suggest a more peaceful motoring era.

Briggate today presents quite a different scene. All traffic has been removed other than for off-peak servicing and pedestrians have full use of the space thus created. This view shows the initial paving and landscaping which is yet to be finalised.

A 1936 view of the east side of Briggate at its junction with Kirkgate. At the extreme right is the former Victory Hotel (with clock) but most of this site was occupied by Hitchens department store, founded late last century. Hitchens ceased trading in 1952 but the site was sold on and remained in similar use by Littlewoods and, latterly Marks and Spencer.

The site was completely redeveloped and enlarged by Littlewoods in the 1960s. Acquisition of the premises of Stead and Simpson enabled the creation of a corner entrance. In 1998 the building was acquired by Marks and Spencer and given a facelift externally and internally (the main M&S store lies just across Briggate).

An early photograph of Briggate's Empire Theatre built at the turn of the century as part of the major shopping development including King Edward and Queen Victoria Streets, Cross and County Arcades. This group is today known as the Victoria Quarter. The Empire was designed by Frank Matcham, the leading Victorian theatre architect.

In the 1960s the Empire was demolished only to be replaced by a new arcade above which were built new offices.

Thirty years later further changes took place when the Harvey Nichols store was built within the outer shell of the old theatre. The only evidence remaining of the Empire Theatre is a plaque to be found at the rear of the store in Cross Arcade. The project received an Award in the Leeds Awards for Architecture 1997, the architects being Brooker Flynn with Hosker, Moore and Kent.

A 1960s view from Briggate looking east down Queen Victoria Street. The street is still open to one-way traffic with parking meters. The flanking buildings originate from the turn of the century, designed by Frank Matcham, leading Victorian theatre architect.

A similar view from 1981 with traffic now excluded to be replaced by the paved pedestrian area.

Queen Victoria Street becomes another fine Leeds Arcade in 1990. The rows of columns create a cathedral like feel and the shops and cafes are flooded with light from the high, glazed roof which features the large modern stained glass mural by Brian Clarke. The overall 1902 development is now known as the Victoria Quarter. The project received an Award in the Leeds Awards for Architecture 1991. The Architect was Derek Latham. The Quarter is listed Grade II*.

A 1984 view looking west along Queen Victoria Street from Vicar Lane, after the initial removal of traffic followed by landscaping. The buildings were erected at the turn of the century as part of the Leeds Estates Company development and designed by Frank Matcham.

In 1990 the owners of the former Estates Company embarked on an ambitious project to restore and improve a whole city block. Prudential Insurance appointed architect Derek Latham to carry out the design and conservation including the creation of a fine glazed arcade by roofing over Queen Victoria Street. The project received an Award in the Leeds Awards for Architecture 1991.

A view from 1944 of the east side of Briggate just north of County Arcade. Bay Horse Yard entry is at the centre of the picture below the oval window, the pub itself did not have a Briggate frontage. The over-sized advertising for the 'Cash Boot Co.' and 'Cash Clothing Co.' was removed just after the war.

A current view showing renovated façades and changes in occupiers. Borders Bookshop lies behind a retained frontage with much more restrained advertising! The small 'Stylo' shop site now features a fashionable fully glazed façade clearly separating the bookshop from the newly restored Victoria Quarter.

The 1960s view looking east down Eastgate with the former Quarry Hill Flats in the background. The flats were built in the late 1930s but demolished forty years later.

Thirty years later, Quarry Hill is dominated by the massive bulk of Quarry House, the building for the Department of Health and Social Security. Just forward of this can be seen the West Yorkshire Playhouse and the former petrol filling station on the Eastgate roundabout. Architects for Quarry House were BDP (Building Design Partnership) and for the Playhouse the Ian Appleton Partnership.

During the nineteenth century the areas to the east of the then town centre became filled with overcrowded housing packed around yards and courts with minimal sanitation. This example is typical of much of the Quarry Hill area. In the 1930s Leeds City Council began clearance of such areas and the building of large housing estates including the Quarry Hill Flats.

A 1960s view of Quarry Hill Flats. This huge slum clearance plan provided over 900 homes and was acclaimed as a masterpiece of municipal planning and design. At the time it was the largest housing development in Europe. The designer was R. A. H. Livett, Architect and Director of Housing for Leeds City Council.

The Flats towards the end of their life in the mid 1970s. The filling station was still functioning despite increasing traffic flows around its perimeter.

The current view shows the new buildings on Quarry Hill. The former petrol station is to be re-modelled forming a Millennium Fountain, having been built in the 1930s as part of the Headrow re-construction scheme (recently listed Grade II). Behind and to its left is Quarry House (Architects – Building Design Partnership). To the right is the West Yorkshire Playhouse which was Commended in the Leeds Awards for Architecture 1990, the Architects being the Ian Appleton Partnership.

Quarry Hill Flats and the crowded Municipal Bus Station as seen from York Street in the mid-1950s. The Flats were constructed with a pioneering light steel frame with pre-cast concrete cladding panels which contrast with the traditional chimneys and flues at the roofline!

Quarry Hill has a very different appearance today with the West Yorkshire Playhouse, Quarry House and the College of Music sited there, with promised further developments. The buildings are set within attractive landscaped gardens. The Bus Station remains, albeit with a much changed layout and the project was Commended in the Leeds Awards for Architecture 1996. The Architects were Abbey Hanson Rowe.

A wartime view of the Headrow from its junction with Briggate. On the north side Lewis's Department Store opened in 1932 and was the largest of its type outside London, costing £1,000,000. The Headrow at this time was open to two-way traffic, though quiet in this view. Note the static water tanks for fire-fighting and the brick blast walls protecting the store entrances

The store is now part of the Allders group and is virtually unchanged externally. The Headrow in this part is now open only to public transport users.

A 1950s view looking north up Lands Lane from the junction with Albion Place. The Theatre Royal, well known for its repertory performances, was replaced in the late 1950s by the expansion of the Schofield's Department Store. Most of the building sites on the left have been re-developed twice in the past 40 years, whilst the buildings on the right remain substantially intact.

Now traffic-free, Lands Lane has the long frontage of the Headrow Centre (formerly Schofield's Centre) on the left. At the head of the street can be seen Allder's Department Store (formerly Lewis's).

A 1960s view from the Headrow looking north up Woodhouse Lane, with Headrow House on the left. The Austin Central Garage was demolished to make way for the St John's Shopping Centre in the 1980s. In the centre of the photo can be seen the Merrion Centre office block, and Tower House (Merrion Way) is on the extreme right.

A substantial area of older buildings was cleared between Albion Street and St John's Church for the new Centre. This area included closing a section of Woodhouse Lane to traffic. Today, part of the area has been laid out as a pedestrian square featuring the Dortmund Drayman statue (unveiled in 1980) celebrating the twinning link with the German city.

This building stood at the junction of the Headrow (*to the left*) and what was Woodhouse Lane, but now forming part of Dortmund Square. Guildford House originated in the mid-nineteenth century but was demolished to make way for the Headrow widening in the early 1930s.

Headrow House was the last building to be erected on the north side of the Headrow, east of Cookridge Street. Opposition to the scheme arose, arguing that the building was excessively high when compared with the original Sir Reginald Blomfield's concept. Plans were approved in 1951 but construction was not completed until 1955. There is a large underground car park, Dortmund Square is on the right.

A 1930 view of the former Schofields Department Store which included the Victoria Arcade of 1898. The store was housed in a variety of old buildings, one of which was the famous Red Hall which was said to have been the first brick building in Leeds. Since this photograph was taken the site has been redeveloped twice.

In the mid-1960s Schofields redeveloped bringing together the various dispersed accommodation into a unified form. Tripe and Wakeham were the architects.

The view from Dortmund Square today with the former Schofields Centre (now the Headrow Centre) to the rear. The architects for the Centre were Crampin and Pring. The building is now a shopping mall on three levels.

Many older buildings in Leeds have continued to serve the community through the years whilst their function has changed from time to time. This group has seen some quite radical changes starting life as the New Connexion Methodist Chapel and Schoolroom in 1858. This 1960s photograph shows the buildings in educational use as the College of Commerce (*left*) and the School of Architecture. The former, *to the left*, is listed Grade II (Architect – William Hill).

The buildings today house functions which would appear to be at conflict with their early Methodist origins, those of the consumption of alcohol! Two separately owned bars and restaurants now occupy the group, one of which is said to be the largest in the country.

A 1960s view of the north side of the Headrow between Calverley Street and Cookridge Street (*on right*). The area known as the Garden of Rest was created in the 1930s when the Headrow was widened. The War Memorial was moved from City Square and lies behind the trees. The Memorial is listed Grade II.

Today the form of the Garden of Rest has been simplified with fewer trees remaining. To the right the former blank gable now forms the new black granite faced entrance into the Henry Moore Sculpture Centre, whose architects were Jeremy Dixon and Edward Jones. The building received an Award in the 1993 Leeds Awards for Architecture.

This photograph was taken in 1928 looking east from the junction of East Parade and what was then Park Lane, now the Headrow. On the extreme left can be seen the Municipal Buildings (Library and Museum) which still exist today. To the extreme right is the Portland stone faced Pearl Chambers. Leeds Permanent Building Society was demolished to make way for the Headrow re-construction and the creation of the Garden of Rest in the 1930s.

A similar view today showing the Garden of Rest and Victoria Square. Beyond the Garden of Rest is Permanent House on Cookridge Street into which the Society relocated in 1930, and which is listed Grade II. The architects for this and the adjoining Headrow frontage were G. W. Atkinson in association with Sir Reginald Blomfield who was responsible for the overall architectural concept.

A 1960s view looking north up Park Street from Westgate. The City Treasury ('Rates Office') is on the left with the former Central Fire Station midway up Park Street on the right. The former University Medical School is seen at the head of the street (on Thoresby Place).

Today Park Street is flanked by two Court buildings, the Magistrate's on the left and the Combined Courts Centre on the right. Large hospital buildings dominate the skyline north of the old Medical School. Architects for the Magistrate's Courts were the Leeds Design Consultancy and for the Courts Centre the Property Services Agency.

A war-time view looking north up East Parade from its junction with Infirmary Street. The buildings still existing today include those just to the left of centre, the Municipal Buildings and Pearl Chambers. This part of Leeds was originally largely occupied by wholesale warehouses (*to the left*) with banking and insurance offices running up to Park Row (*to the right*).

Today's view is very different with the scene dominated by modern office buildings largely given over to banking, insurance and legal firms.

The former Prudential offices designed by Alfred Waterhouse (1894); this view from early this century taken from South Parade. The cost was £600,000 and it was the first Leeds building to have lifts (listed Grade II).

This view from the early 1980s shows how much of the building's character had been lost by changes to the roofline.

Now known as Park Row House, the building was sensitively restored and renovated by Abbey Hanson Rowe, Architects. The project was Commended in the 1992 Leeds Awards for Architecture.

This view is from 1944, taken from the junction with Bond Street, and the location of the first traffic lights in Britain in 1928. On the right is Beckett's Bank by Gilbert Scott (1867), sadly lost in the post-war building boom. Opposite is the former Williams, Brown and Co's Bank designed by Alfred Waterhouse (1898), listed Grade II.

A current view showing radical changes to the east side of Park Row (and to traffic patterns!). Fifty years on further changes are likely to this street scene of Park Row, hopefully improving its architectural and urban quality.

The Leeds Museum and Philosophical Hall once stood on Park Row (running across foreground) at its junction with Bond Street, this view from early this century.

Enemy bombing in the early 1940s destroyed the Park Row frontage and a temporary entrance was formed, across a small garden. This view from 1966.

In the early 1970s the old building was replaced by the Midland Bank and offices (now HSBC), seen from across Park Row. To the rear of the Bank is Bond Court the open space around which offices and car park were built in the mid-1960s as part of Leeds City Council's first Comprehensive Development Area.

The New Basin, or Clarence Dock, was built around 1840, greatly increasing the wharfage for commercial barge traffic. The post-war demise of this witnessed the wharves and goods depots becoming derelict as seen in this 1979 photograph.

The Royal Armouries Museum forms the centre-piece in the proposals to revitalise Clarence Dock. Designed by Derek Walker Associates it was opened in 1996, the first stage of a projected mixed use development that will surround the dock. At its north end is the fully-glazed Hall of Steel with its mass display of over 4,000 weapons and armour. The Museum received an Award in the Leeds Awards for Architecture 1996.

A 1960s view from Crown Point Bridge looking east. St Saviour's Church, the riverside former flax mills and the Sea Cadet Corps HQ remain today, but much clearance took place downstream on the right.

The revitalised scene today with the Royal Armouries Museum dominating the south bank of the Aire. The Sea Cadets HQ has been given a facelift and much redevelopment has taken place on the north bank including the attractive conversion to offices of the former flax mills.

A 1970s view looking across the river to the north bank, just south of the Parish Church. The area was largely in industrial usage, much of it in a very poor condition. To the left a former concrete coal staithe was in use by a builders merchant.

In 1986 the site was re-developed as the 'Chandlers' by a housing association providing 120 flats, partly new-build and partly within the former Turtons Crown Point Provender Mills of 1876 (access from The Calls). It was the first riverside development forming part of the City Council's Riverside 'Plan of Action'. This pioneer scheme was originally built for rent but well over 50% has now been sold. An important element of the project was the provision of a public riverside walkway. Architects were Denison Peters Ltd, the scheme receiving a Commendation in the Leeds Awards for Architecture 1988.

A 1970s view from Crown Point Bridge looking west indicates the former industrial nature of the banks of the Aire. Many of the buildings were falling into disrepair and investment was urgently needed.

Investment in quite a different way came along with the change from industrial use to a largely residential role in the early 1990s. Langton's Wharf with 67 apartments can be seen with the Design Innovation Centre upstream to its left. The latter was converted from a 1930s grain and flour warehouse. Langtons Wharf was developed by Taylor Woodrow/Hillstar whilst the Architects for the Design Centre were Allen Tod. The Centre received an Award in the Leeds Awards for Architecture 1989.

The view looking north over the Aire from the former Aire and Calder Navigation's 1821 basin, now part of Victoria Quay's housing development. Fletland Mills the three-gabled block just west of the 1992 Centenary footbridge had fallen into disrepair together with much of its riverside surroundings.

Fletland Mills, originating from the late eighteenth century, was transformed into a high-class hotel with international restaurant. '42, The Calls' was opened in 1990–91 and received an Award in the Leeds Awards for Architecture 1992, the architects being Allen Tod, acting for 'A Way of Life', Ltd.

A view looking west from the south bank of the Aire, midway between the Leeds and Victoria bridges shows the dereliction to be found in the area in the 1960s. The only structures that remain today are Victoria Bridge, former Canal Warehouse and the Italianate Towers

Today's view shows the Embankment group of office buildings (1991–1994) which front the riverside from the converted Victoria Mills to Neville Street to the west. A restaurant occupies the ground floor of part of the former. Overall the project provides 100,000 sq. ft. of accommodation.

A view of the Embankment group from Victoria Bridge, Neville Street. In a variety of architectural styles mainly in brick, the project has extensive landscaping, riverside walkways and terraces. The prestigious accommodation includes KPMG, Yorkshire Water, DTZ Debenham Thorpe and Countryside Commission. Developers were St James Securities with David Lyons Associates, Architects.

This 1960s view from the south bank of the Aire just west of Victoria Bridge (Neville Street) shows the former Dragonara Hotel (now Hilton) towering over the former coal depot of the Leeds Co-op. Note the moored barges, coal staithes and steam crane. Leeds City Station is in left background.

Victoria Gate, the attractive new building for Privilege Insurance now occupies the former coal depot site. The Hilton National Hotel can just be seen above the new building with Neville Street on the right of the photograph. The building was Commended in the Leeds Awards for Architecture 1998, the Architects being the T. P. Bennett Partnership.

Leeds Civic Hall, Calverley Street

This was opened by King George V in 1933, after a public works programme to ease unemployment during the depression. The architect was E. Vincent Harris who was responsible for many other contemporary civic buildings around the country. Controversy arose at the time because of the use of white Portland stone contrasting with the (then) black Town Hall. Recently cleaned it has some of the qualities of an expensive wedding cake. Its twin pinnacles are surmounted by seven foot high gilded owls.

Its overall design with thin, widely spaced towers has not always received critical acclaim but today is seen as much of a symbol of civic pride as the Town Hall.

As one eminent critic puts it '. . . the Civic Hall is as ambitious as the Town Hall but not as self confident.' (Listed Grade II*)

Brotherton Wing
Leeds General Infirmary (1936), Calverley Street.

Combined Courts Centre (1972), Headrow and Oxford Row. Architects – Property Services Agency.

Henry Moore Gallery Extension to City Art Gallery (1980), Architects – Leeds City council.

The Royal Armouries Museum (1996), Waterfront. Architects – Derek Walker Associates. Award in Leeds Awards for Architecture (L.A.A.) 1996.

St Anne's Roman Catholic Cathedral, Cookridge Street

The present building replaced one at the junction of the Headrow and Cookridge Street which was removed late last century for road widening. The Cathedral was built 1902–1904 by Architects J. H. Eastwood and Sydney Greenslade in the Arts and Crafts style. Much of the fine detailing is reminiscent of the work of Charles Rennie Mackintosh. The interior is spacious but externally its cramped sloping site does not enhance its setting. However, some wonderful craftsmanship in masonry and sculpture can be enjoyed, particularly at high level (listed Grade II*).

Oxford Place Chapel
Danby and Thorp, 1896–1903
(Listed Grade II)

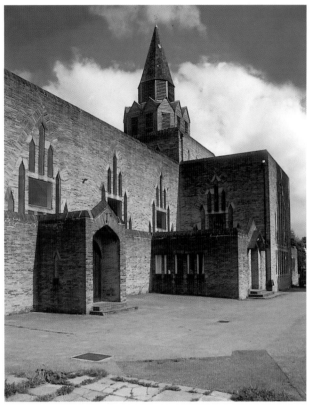

St Wilfred
Halton, 1938
Architect – A. Randall-Wells
(Listed Grade II)

Church of the Epiphany
Gipton, 1938
Architect – N. F. Cachemaille-Day
(Listed Grade I)

Church of St Paul the Apostle
Alwoodley, 1998
Architects – Edwin Trotter Associates
Commended L.A.A. 1998

No. 16 Park Row is a striking addition to the local streetscape in contrast with its more sober (and solid) neighbours. A sheer wall of plate-glass rises from pavement level enclosing a narrow atrium. A computer controlled coloured illumination system enhances the building by night. Carey Jones were the architects and the building was Commended in the Leeds Awards for Architecture 1997.

By contrast, **Apsley House**, Wellington Street was built in 1903, a substantial structure in brick and terracotta. Though employing contemporary materials the building displays many design elements and features to be found in later structures. The influences of the Chicago School of design are evident in the window styling and the substantial daylighting available from the light and airy façades (listed Grade II).

Atlas Chambers
King Street, 1910
Architects – Perkin and Bulmer
Entrance detail

East Parade Chambers
1899
Entrance detail
(Listed Grade II)

Crispin House
New York Road, 1916
(formerly H. and W. Heaton's clothing
factory)
(Listed Grade II)

City Station Concourse
City Square, 1938
Architects for restoration in 1999 – Carey
Jones

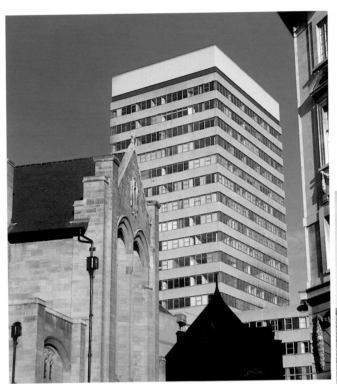

Dudley House
Albion Street, 1969

Westgate Point
Westgate, 1988
Architects – David Lyons and associates
Commended in L.A.A. 1989

Eagle Star
1 East Parade, 1994
Architects – William Gower Partnership

No. 1 Park Row
City Square, 1997
Architects – Fletcher Joseph

The Bourse
Off Boar Lane, 1993
Architects – Sir Basil Spence Partnership
Commended in L.A.A. 1994

Offices
Trevelyan Square and Boar Lane, 1992
Architects – Chapman Taylor & Partners
Commended in L.A.A. 1993

Quarry House
Marsh Lane, 1990
Architects – Building Design Partnership

Sovereign House
Sovereign Street, 1997
Architects – Knott Mercer Partnership

The stylish tower of **Lloyds Bank** at the junction of Park Row and Bond Street was opened in 1976 (now known as Lloyds TSB). This is a building of quality that fits its corner site very well on a raised podium. Set beneath the overhang is Peter Tysoe's famous Black Horse sculpture in steel. Architects were Abbey Hanson Rowe.

By contrast with Lloyds, banking earlier this century was carried on at a much more modest scale. Leeds has several older surviving banks, some in their original use. **Abtech House**, No. 18 Park Row (and close to Lloyds) was originally the West Riding Union Bank designed by E. J. Dodgshun and opened in 1900. This bank also has decorative sculpture, an attractive frieze on which the international nature of banking at the time is depicted. This beautiful example was by Joseph Thewlis (listed Grade II).

The former Midland Bank
City Square, 1899 (now a bar-restaurant)
Architect – W. W. Gwyther
Listed Grade II

Yorkshire Bank
Kirkgate, 1900

Former Bank of England
South Parade, 1864 (now offices and bar)
Architect – Philip Hardwick
Listed Grade II

Bank of England
King Street, 1967
Architects – Building Design Partnership

The University of Leeds was founded in the 1880s, the main buildings being opened by the Prince of Wales in 1885, including those designed by the nationally-known architect Alfred Waterhouse. Beginning in the late 1920s another phase of development took place, designed by architects Lanchester and Lodge. The Parkinson Building on Woodhouse Lane is a well-known city landmark, its tower sited on a high point to the north of the city centre. In a neo-classic style and faced in Portland stone this building, though started just before World War Two, was not completed until 1951 (listed Grade II).

In the early 1960s there was a considerable expansion of University facilities with a master-plan designed by architects Chamberlin, Powell and Bon. This time the material to be used was the then-fashionable reinforced concrete. The unusual building illustrated is the central lecture theatre block which forms the centrepiece of the huge Chancellors Court.

Gower Street Board School
1886 (now partially in use as restaurant)

Former Pupil Teachers Centre
Great George Street, 1900
(then City of Leeds School and converted into
council offices in 1995 by Leeds Design Consultancy) –
Listed Grade II

Carr Manor Centre
Stainbeck Lane, 1937
(formerly Stainbeck School)

Roundhay School
Old Park Road, 1920

Leeds College of Art
Cookridge Street, 1903
Architects – Bedford and Kitson
(Listed Grade II*)

Brunswick Building
Leeds Metropolitan University, 1978
Leeds City Architect

Northern School of Contemporary Dance
Chapeltown Road
(formerly United Hebrew Congregation Synagogue, 1930
by J. Stanley Wright.)
Architects for the changes in 1998 were Allen Tod
(Listed Grade II)

Leeds College of Art and Design
(formerly Jacob Kramer College, 1981
Blenheim Walk – Leeds City Architect

The County Arcade, Victoria Quarter

An area of narrow yards and courts, butchers shops and gruesome slaughter houses was bought up, demolished and redeveloped by the Leeds Estates Company in 1897–1902. Frank Matcham, recognised as the best theatre architect of this period used a combination of lavish materials to create two streets, two arcades and the Empire Theatre. The County Arcade is of unrivalled quality, the fine mahogany shop fronts separated by pink marble columns. Ample daylight is provided by the ornate glass and iron roof and the floor is an excellent example of modern mosaic work. The County Arcade has been recently restored and renovated as part of the Victoria Quarter. The Architect was Derek Latham and the scheme received an Award in the Leeds Awards for Architecture 1991 (Listed Grade II*).

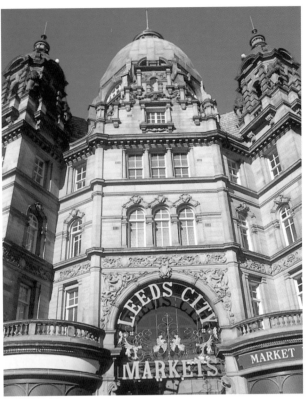

Kirkgate Markets
Leeming and Leeming, 1904
Restoration in 1994
Architects – Povall Worthington
Commended in L.A.A. 1994 (Listed Grade I)

Corn Exchange Shops
Cuthbert Brodrick, 1862
Conversion in 1990
Architect – John Lyall
Award in L.A.A. 1990 (Listed Grade I)

Debenhams
Briggate, 1936 – Conversion in 1998 by
Architects – Carey Jones

Fish Bar
Roundhay Road, Oakwood, 1937
(Listed Grade II – Shop front)

Merrion Centre – Woodhouse Lane, 1960–1970, Architects – Gillinson Barnett & Allen

Sainsbury's Supermarket – Moor Allerton, 1998 – Architects – Chetwood Associates

Headrow Centre
(formerly Schofields), 1984
Architects – Crampin & Pring

White Rose Centre
Churwell, 1998
Architects – Building Design Partnership
Award for Landscape, L.A.A., 1998

The **Metropole Hotel**, King Street, presents a tour de force in brick, terracotta and faience. Opened in 1899 it was built close to the railway stations and business areas. The stone cupola at roof level originally crowned the Fourth White Cloth Hall on whose site the Hotel was built (listed Grade II). The architects were Chorley and Connon.

The entrance to the Metropole shows something of the ornate details that were possible when creating moulds for terracotta. Very fine and intricate decoration in an 'Art nouveau' style can be seen on the frontage..

The **Queen's Hotel**, City Square, was opened in 1937, replacing an earlier railway hotel from last century. It has a massive Portland stone façade screening the City Station from the Square. It was one of a handful of 1930s buildings in Leeds which employed this material, others, including the Civic Hall and University. The architect was W. Curtis Green (listed Grade II).

The Malmaison
Swinegate, 1999
(Conversion of former City Transport offices)
Architects for conversion – Ferrier Crawford Partnership

42, The Calls and Waterfront
1991
(Conversion of former Fletland Mills)
Architects – Allen Tod
Award in L.A.A. 1992

Crowne Plaza Hotel
Wellington Street, 1993
Architects – D. J. Curtis and Associates

Marriott Hotel
Trevelyan Square, off Boar Lane, 1994
Architects – Cobban and Lironi

The changes in one particular building type through the century are highlighted on this page. Cinemas were something quite new without architectural precedents and their style, particularly between the Great Wars, often bordered on the exotic.

The Hyde Park Picture House, Brudenell Road, built in 1908, and a rare survival from the early years of moving pictures. It is one of only three 'traditional' suburban cinemas still operating in Leeds (Listed Grade II). The architects were Thomas Winn and Sons.

The former **Clock Cinema**, Roundhay Road is now in shopping use (1938). Probably the best example of the 'Art Moderne' or 'Art Deco' cinemas in the city. Many others designed in such styles were lost in the 1960s and 1970s. The architects were Kitson, Parish, Ledgard and Pyman.

Warner Bros. Village, Multiplex Cinemas, Kirkstall Road (1997), is the latest approach to 'movie' entertainment, offering patrons a wide choice of films. It forms part of a larger leisure and entertainment complex (architects – Benoy Associates).

The West Yorkshire Playhouse
Quarry Hill, 1989
Architects – Ian Appleton Partnership
Commended in L.A.A. 1990

Bramley Baths
Broad Lane, 1904
(Listed Grade II)

Tetley's Brewery Wharf
Waterfront, 1993
Architects – Carey Jones Seifert
Commended in L.A.A. 1994

Alwoodley Golf Club
Wigton Lane, 1994
Designer – Charles Morris, Chartered Surveyor
Commended in L.A.A. 1995